Billions of Bats

Miriam Schlein

BILLIONS OF BATS

illustrated by Walter Kessell

J.B. Lippincott   New York

Library of Congress Cataloging in Publication Data

Schlein, Miriam.
Summary: Discusses several unusual varieties of
the more than 800 different kinds of bats, such as
the vampire bat, the flying fox, the tomb bat, and
the sword-nosed bat.
1. Bats—Juvenile literature. [1. Bats]
I. Kessell, Walter, ill, II. Title.
QL737.C5S34 1982   599.4   81-47752
ISBN 0-397-31984-3   AACR2
ISBN 0-397-31985-1 (lib. bdg.)
1   2   3   4   5   6   7   8   9   10
FIRST EDITION

Billions of Bats

Suppose you're walking along, and your friend says: "I just saw a mouse fly by!"

Would you believe—a flying mouse?

There is no such thing as a mouse that flies. There is only one mammal in the world that can fly—and it's not a mouse. But it has a small furry body, like a mouse. And it looks so much like one, that in many countries it is called "the flying mouse."

It is—the bat.

A bat doesn't have feathery wings like a bird's. It has wings made of skin. They're very big wings, and they're attached to practically every part of the bat's body—its back and belly, its legs and tail; even to its hands and fingers.

Did you know bats have fingers? They're unusual fingers. They're very long. But a bat can't pick up anything with these fingers, because they're totally embedded in the wing (except for the thumb, which has a little claw sticking out).

Still, the fingers are important. They support and spread out the bat's big wings.

Have you ever seen a bat?

There are more than 800 different species of bats. They live everywhere in the world except for Antarctica, the North Arctic, and

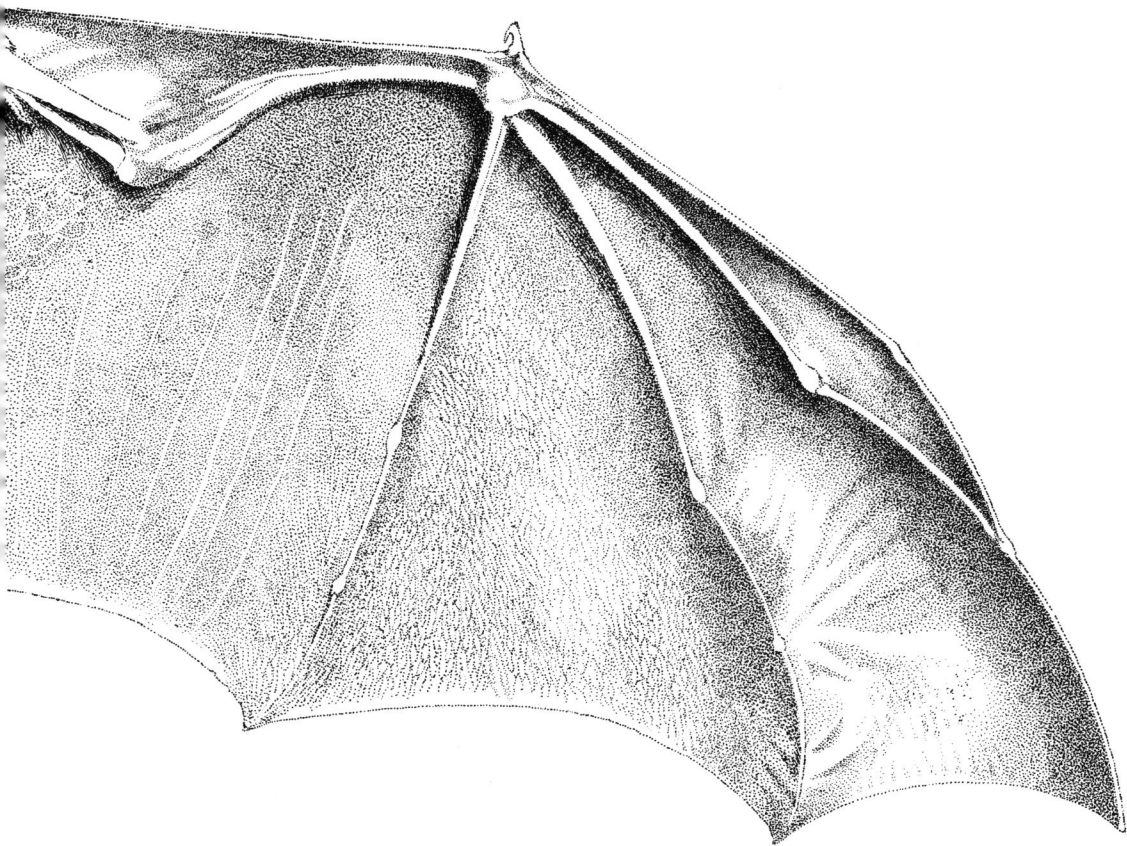

a few scattered islands in the oceans.

So, there are probably bats not too far from where you live. If you have never seen one, maybe this is why.

Most bats fly around only at night. In the daytime, they hang upside down by their toes and sleep. The place where they do this is called their *roost.*

Bats usually roost in dark, hidden-away places. In caves and sewers. In mines and wells no longer being used. Under the edge of the roof of a house. Some roost alone. Others roost in large groups—thousands, or even millions all together. Some roost in trees.

One kind of bat that lives all over the United States is the Red Bat. You could walk right past a tree with Red Bats roosting in it and not even notice them. They're a

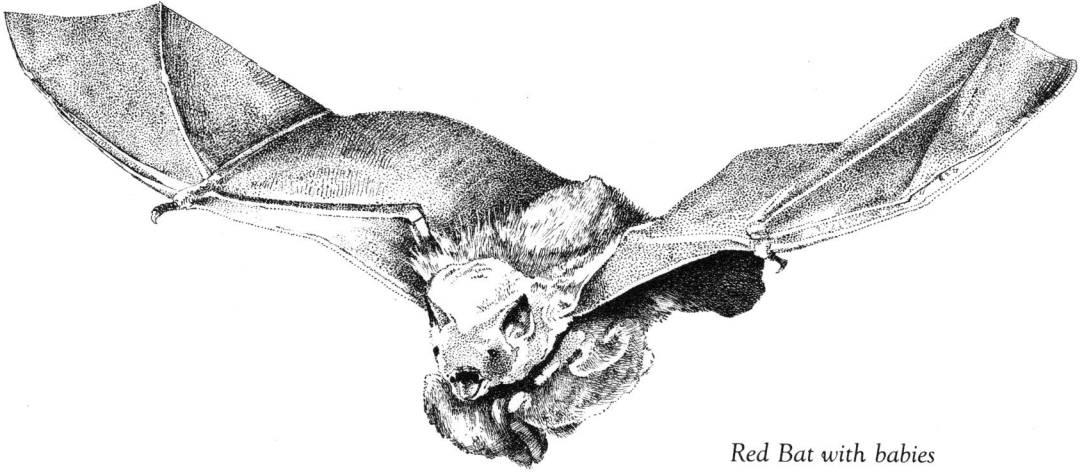

Red Bat with babies

rusty color, and are only about 3 inches long. They look like dry leaves hanging there. Still, they're good flyers. They can fly 13 miles an hour.

Most bats have just one baby bat at a time. Red Bats are different. A Red Bat mother has 2 or 3 or 4 baby bats at a time. When they're young, the babies hang on-to her as she flies around. Sometimes all the babies together weigh more than the mother herself.

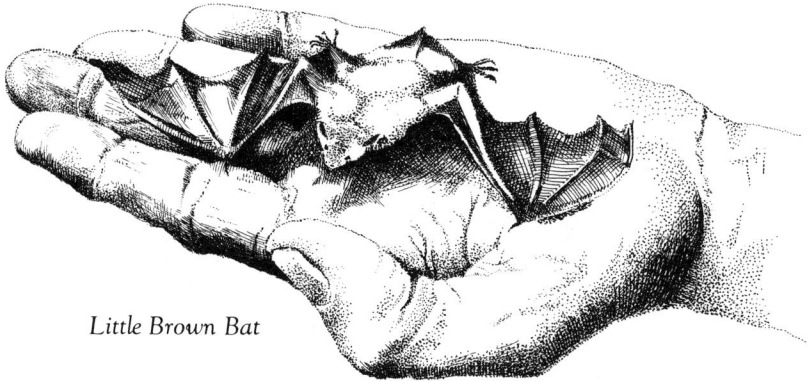
Little Brown Bat

Living everywhere in the United States is another kind of bat called the Little Brown Bat. Some types are 2 or 3 inches long. Others are even more tiny. Their head and body measure little more than 1 inch. Six of them together will weigh about 1 ounce.

Little Brown Bats are born in spring and summer. At that time, the mother bats all roost together in a group, away from the male bats. This is called a *maternity colony*. Sometimes there are 10,000 bats in one colony.

Red Bats and Little Brown Bats eat insects. Some bats eat other things.

*Close-up view
of Little Brown Bat*

A Flying Cow?

Here's a bat with a funny name. It's called the Little Flying Cow. The Little Flying Cow eats flowers.

This bat lives in Africa, in the tops of tall trees. It's called a little flying "cow" because people think its face looks like the face of a young calf.

In the daytime, it roosts in the treetops. When it begins to get dark, the Little Flying Cow comes down to eat. If you watched one, this is what you'd see.

First, she hangs onto a flower with her little

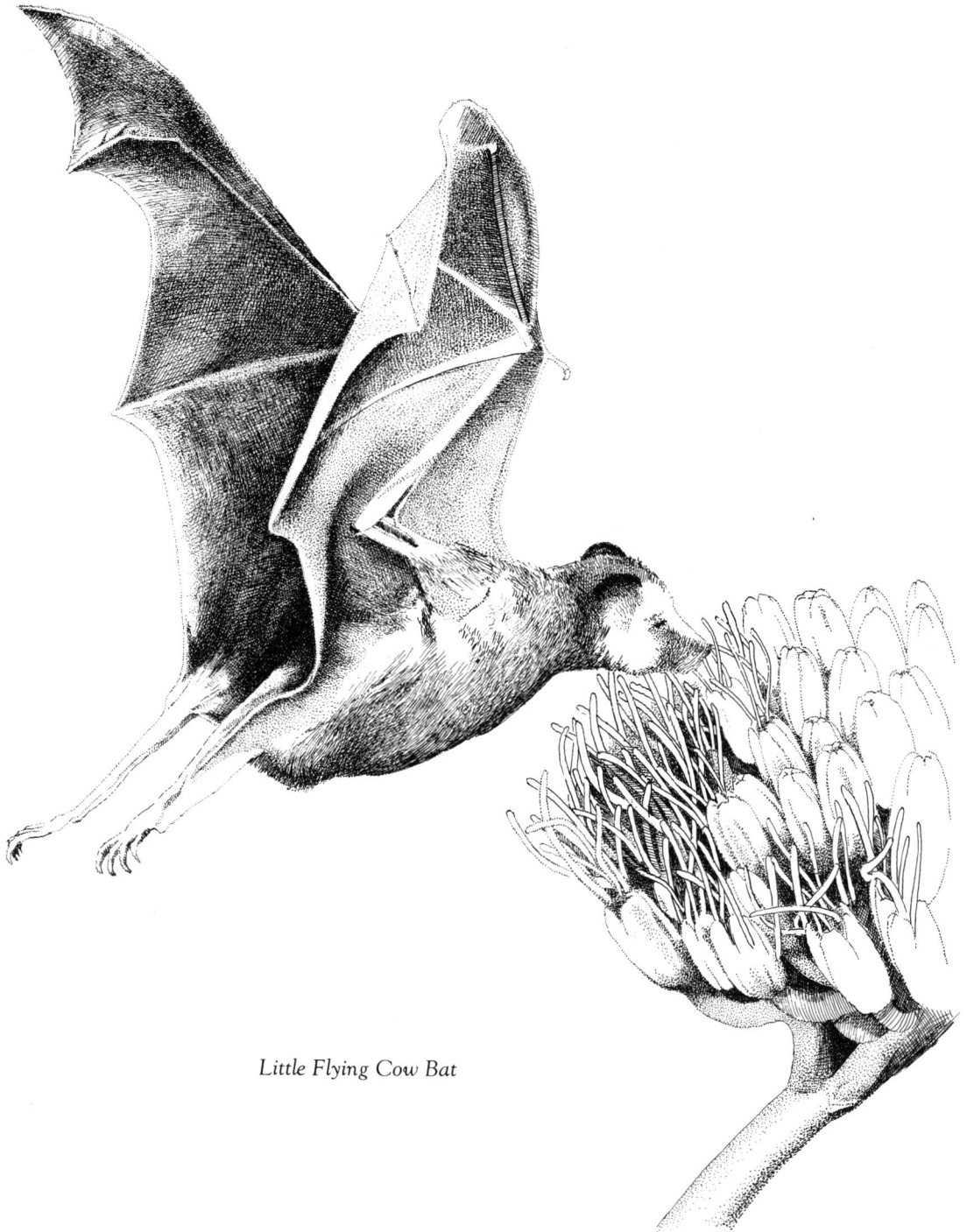

Little Flying Cow Bat

thumb claw. Then she sticks her face down in the middle of the flower. She doesn't eat the flower itself. But she uses her tongue to lap up the flower's sweet liquid, called nectar.

When she's finished at one flower, she throws herself off in a back flip, spreads her wings, and flies off to another flower.

Sometimes she stays on a flower for just one second. Sometimes for thirty seconds. She goes from flower to flower this way all night. Then, before it gets light, she flies back up to the treetops to sleep and rest all day, hanging upside down by her toes.

Many bats feed on flowers. They all have very long rough tongues with little hairs at the tip. The hairs help them to lick up the nectar. Some bats also eat pollen—the tiny dust-like specks you see in the center of flowers.

Little Flying Cows are about 3 inches long.

The Bat that
Drinks Fresh Blood

Have you ever heard of a vampire? It's supposed to be the ghost of someone dead that rises from the grave at night, and kills people by sucking their blood.

In real life there is no such thing as a vampire person. They're only in made-up stories, or on TV.

But there is such a thing as a Vampire Bat. They're small. About 3 inches long. They weigh less than an ounce.

Vampire bats live on only one kind of food. Fresh blood.

Like most bats, vampire bats sleep in the day in some dark place, hanging upside down by their toes. They only come out when it's very dark. Then they leave their roost and fly around, looking for some animal that's sleeping outside, such as a horse, a cow, a donkey, or even a chicken.

When they see one, they land near it. Then, walking on feet and thumbs, the vampire bat climbs up on the animal and bites it.

It's a very small bite—only about a tenth of an inch long. It doesn't hurt. The animal usually doesn't even wake up.

After making the bite, the vampire bat makes

Vampire Bat walking

a funnel by curving its tongue. Then it sucks in, and the blood flows along its tongue and down its throat.

The vampire bat usually sucks for about a half hour. When it's finished, it can hardly fly away, it's so heavy with blood.

Vampires roost alone, or in small groups, or sometimes in large groups of thousands all together in a big dark cave. The cave will then have a strong smell, like ammonia, from all the digested blood dripping down.

Once in a while, a vampire bat will drink blood from a human being. An animal or a human will not die from the loss of blood, because the small vampire bat doesn't drink that much. But there is the danger of getting a bad infection or even rabies (which can kill you) from a bad bite.

Vampire bats live in parts of Mexico and

Close-up view
of Vampire Bat

down throughout South America. There are none in Europe, Africa or Asia. And there are none in the United States.

So, if you go camping out in the United States, you don't have to worry about being bitten by a vampire bat. You don't have to worry about your dog, either, if it sleeps out in a doghouse. In fact, even in countries where there *are* vampire bats, dogs usually do not get bitten by them.

Do you know why?

It's because dogs have such good hearing.

As a vampire bat flies along, it makes very high squeaking sounds through its nose and mouth. This kind of super-high sound is called ultrasound. Humans are not able to hear these ultrasonic bat sounds. But a dog can hear them. The sounds will wake him up, and the vampire bat will not attack.

Horses, goats, and other animals do not have as good hearing as dogs. That is why they are the usual victims of the vampire bat.

Flying in the Dark

It's not just vampire bats that make these ultrasonic sounds as they fly. Most bats do it—and for a very good reason. It's the way they find their way around in the dark.

People sometimes say: "blind as a bat." It's not true. Bats are not blind. But it *is* true that most bats do not use their eyes to guide themselves. Instead, they use their ears and noses and mouths in a special way. It's called *echo-location*.

This is how it works.

18

The bat flies along, making these ultrasonic sounds through his mouth and nose. When there is something ahead in the dark, the sounds hit it, and the echo bounces back to the bat. The bat hears the echo, and he knows that something is there. What's more, the bat can tell if the object ahead of him is a tree, or rock, or just a little insect flying along. Different things make different kinds of echoes, and the bat can recognize them.

Many bats eat insects—things like beetles, spiders, scorpions and moths. By using echo-location, a bat can catch a moth in midair, even in total darkness.

As he flies along, the bat keeps turning his head from side to side, sending out a beam of sound. When the sound hits the body of the moth, the echo bounces back to the bat.

He can pinpoint the position of the flying

moth, swoop down in a nose dive, and catch it in his wing. Then he tucks the rear part of his wing under his body to make a little "lap," and carries the moth back to his roost, where he eats it. Or, sometimes he just eats it as he flies along.

Have you ever seen a bat close-up?

Look at the nose and ears, and you will see some things that help it do its echo-location.

What is that funny thing on the nose?

It is called a *nose-leaf*. It is made of flesh and grows out from the nose. Bat experts think the nose-leaf probably helps to direct the sounds the bat sends out.

Many bats have nose-leaves. But not all of them do. A Tomb Bat has no nose-leaf. But it is still able to echo-locate and catch small flying insects.

Triple Nose-leaf Bat
of Iran and Egypt

Tomb Bat of Africa, Asia, and Australia

Look at more close-ups. What else do you notice?

Lots of bats have super-big ears. This also helps in echo-location, because big ears catch sound better.

Sword-nosed bat of
Mexico and South America

Mexican Big-eared Bat of
Southwestern United States
and Mexico

Long-eared Bat of
United States and southern Canada

Look at the bat named the Long-eared Bat. Its ears are about 2 inches high. This is huge—considering that the bat itself is only 2 or 3 inches long.

As the Long-eared Bat hunts for food, these big ears are pointed forward. It can catch moths in mid-air, and it can hunt in another way, too. It can hover like a hummingbird as it plucks hidden insects out of leafy trees and bushes. The Long-eared Bat's ears are so big that he curls them up when he roosts.

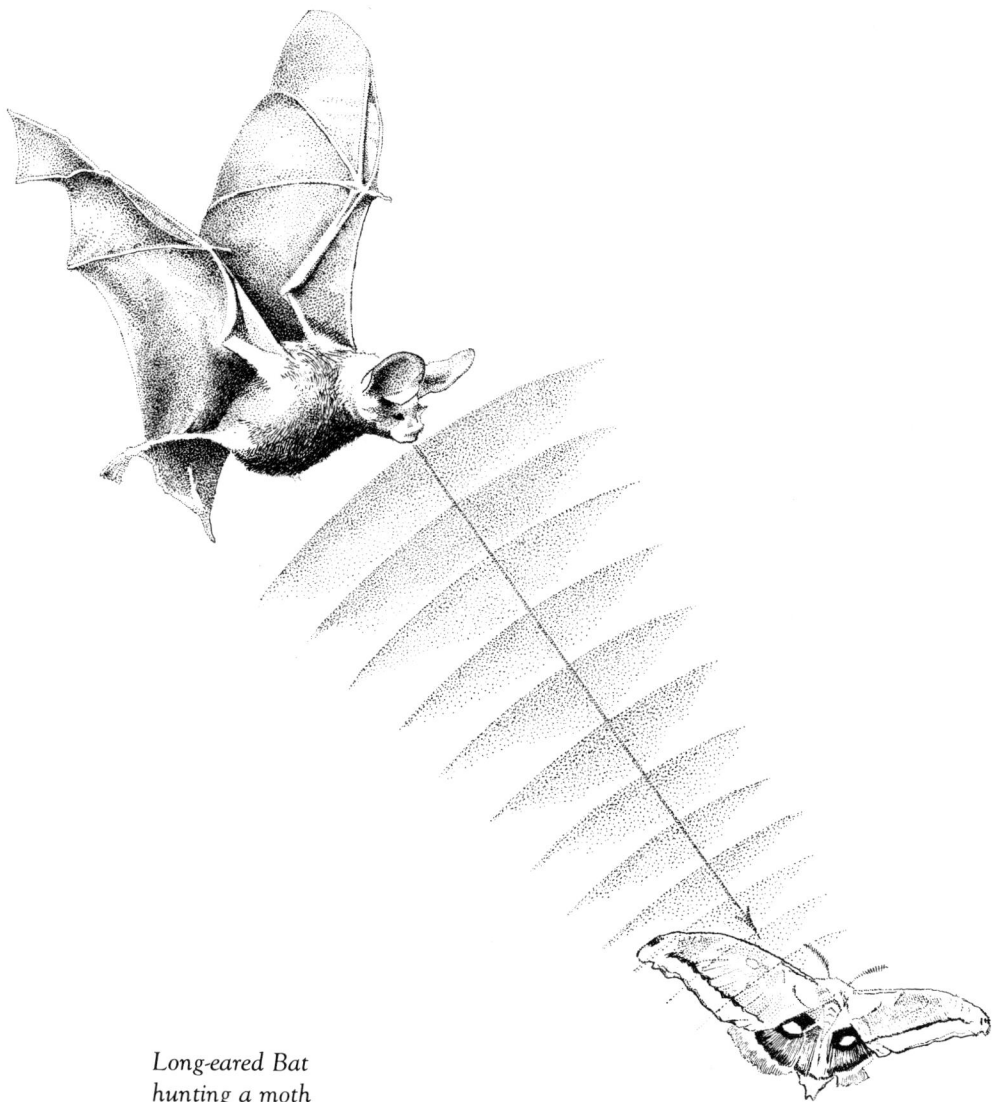

*Long-eared Bat
hunting a moth*

Now look at the thing in front of the ear. It is also made of skin, and is called a *tragus*. People who study bats think the tragus helps to pinpoint the direction that the echoes are coming from as the bats do their echolocation.

There is one more special thing about the ear, but you can't see it. It's inside the ear. It's a tiny muscle. At the moment the bat makes his own ultrasonic sound, this muscle closes up the ear. This is so the bat will not confuse the sound he is making himself with the echo he is listening for.

As bats fly by in the dark, it's not easy to get a good look at them. So, many people think all bats look pretty much the same.

But is that true? Not really.

Each species is, in some way, just a little bit different from the others. And some are *very* different.

26

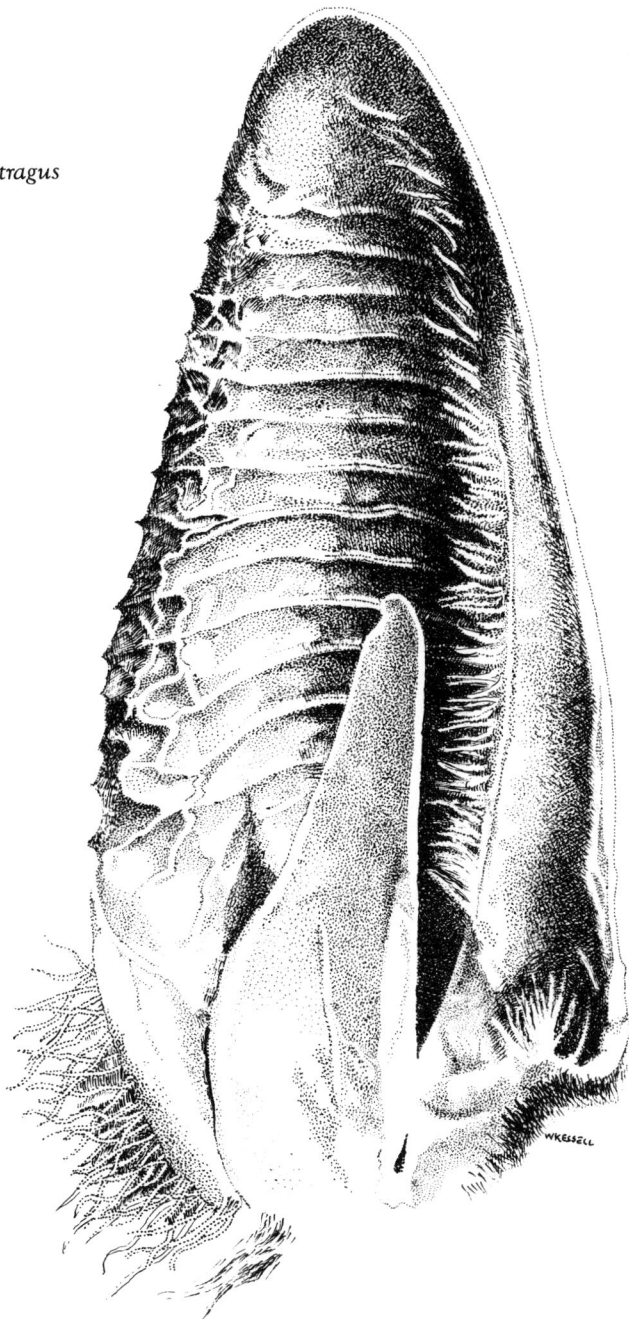

Detail
of Long-eared Bat's tragus

Naked Bat

Spotted (or Pinto) Bat
of western United States and
Mexico

Most bats are furry. But there is one called the Naked Bat, with no fur—just a few little hairs on its face and neck, and that's all. Naked Bats live in Borneo and the Philippines.

Most bats are little brown or gray things. But some have orange fur. Some have spots. Some have stripes on their faces.

Most bats come out only at night. But Butterfly Bats fly around in bright daylight! These 2-inch bats have spots on their wings, and can hover in the air like butterflies. They live in Africa, and roost in banana leaves.

One bat builds a tiny house. He is called the Tent Building Bat. He bites the edge of a palm leaf so it hangs down. This protects him from the wind, the rain, and the sun. Tent Building Bats are found from Mexico down to Brazil.

There are bats that catch fish with their long toes as they zigzag over the water. If they fall in, there's no problem, because they swim with their wings. These are called Fisherman Bats. They live in Mexico and down through South America.

Fisherman Bat
catching fish

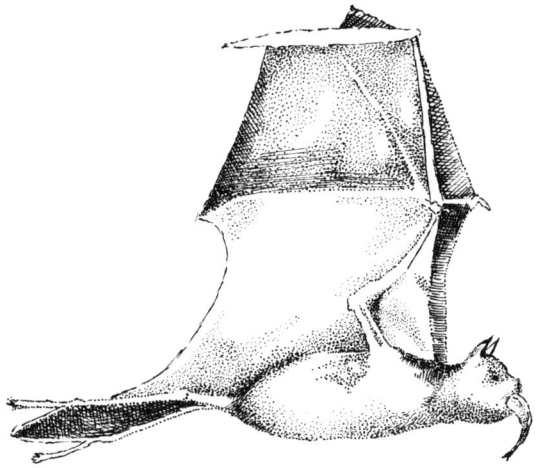

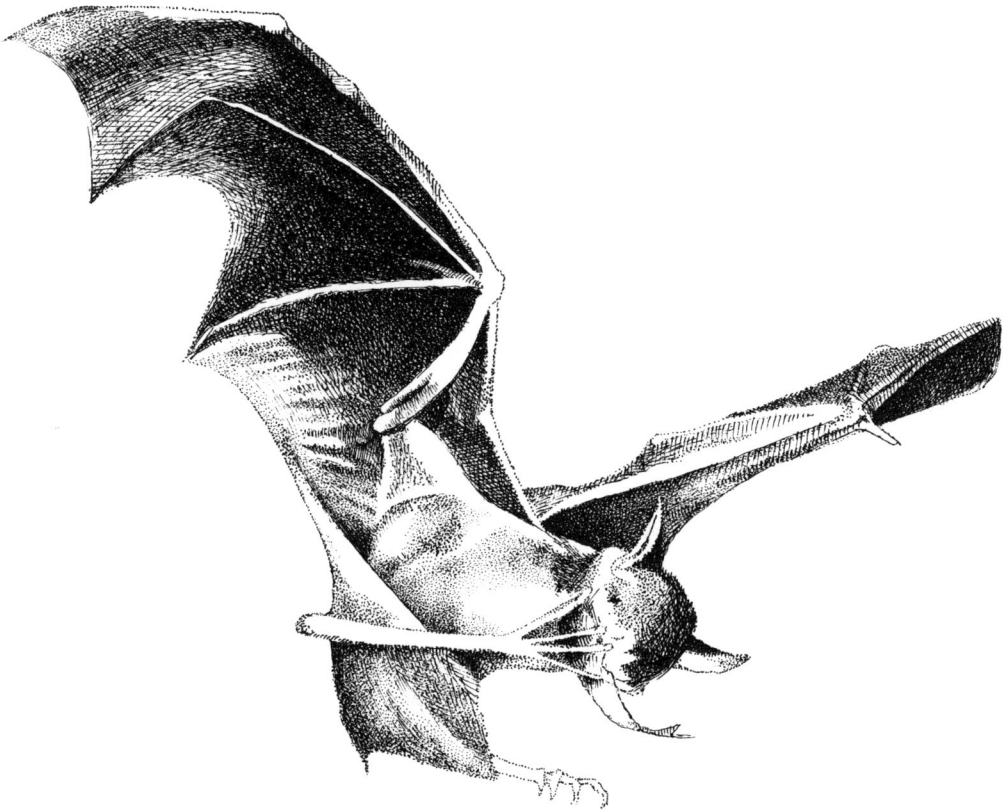

There's an Australian bat called the Ghost Bat. The thing that's different about them is their diet. They're meat-eaters. They eat birds, frogs, small mammals, and even other bats. Ghost Bats are about 5 inches long, and have very pale fur—almost white, like a ghost.

There is a bat that has little suction cups on its ankles and wrists that help it to cling to a smooth leaf. It's name is the Sucker-footed Bat. It is different in another way. It hangs head up by its thumbs, instead of upside down by its toes. The Sucker-footed Bat lives in South America. It is sometimes called The Disk-winged Bat.

The Slit-faced Bat has a sort of crack down the middle of its face. But the most interesting thing is not its face, but its tail. No other animal in the world has a tail like it.

It has a tail that is T-shaped. It ends in *two* tips. They don't hang out, though. Like most bat tails, the tail is embedded in the rear part of the wing.

Slit-faced Bats live in Israel, Egypt, and other parts of the Middle East. They eat butterflies, moths, spiders, and scorpions. They roost in caves, old aardvark burrows, trees, and rooftops. They are sometimes called Hollow-faced Bats.

Sometimes Slit-faced Bats roost together with another kind of bat that has an interesting tail. This is the Mouse-tailed Bat. Most bats have tails that are sort of built into the rear wing. But Mouse-tailed Bats have tails that hang out behind the wing. Mouse-tailed Bats sometimes hang by their thumbs, instead of their toes. They often roost in pyramids.

Mouse-tailed Bat

What's that thing hanging in the tree? Is it a cocoon?

Look closely. You will see it is hanging by two little feet.

It's a roosting Horseshoe Bat.

Most bats, when they roost, tuck their wings to their sides. Others wrap them around the body, letting their head stick out. But a Horseshoe Bat wraps its wings all around itself. You can't see any part of it, except those little feet.

Some Horseshoe Bats are only about 1 inch long. They're so tiny and light, you could hold 7 or 8 in one hand. Altogether, they will weigh about 1 ounce.

Horseshoe Bat

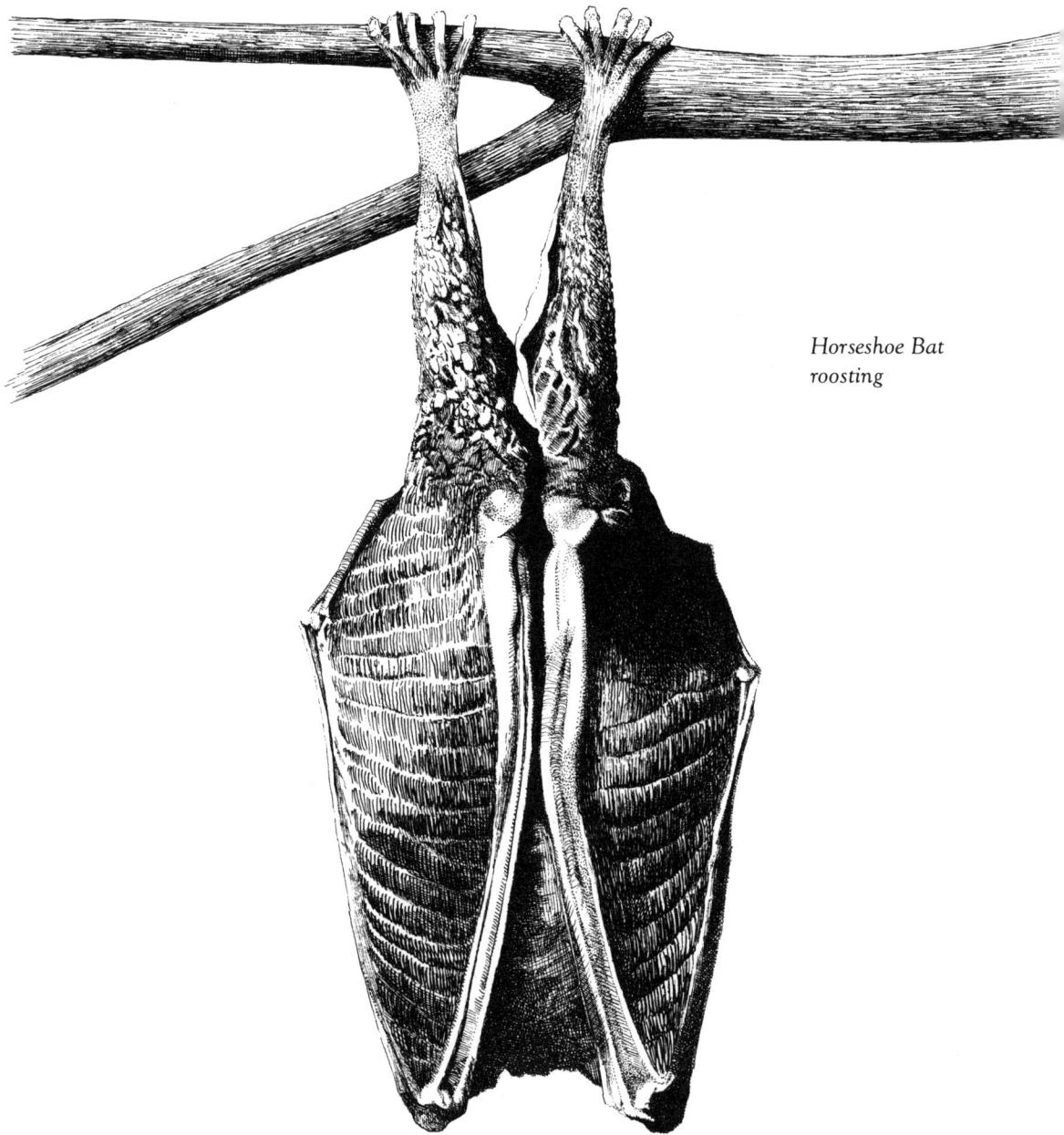

Horseshoe Bat
roosting

Here is a riddle for you.

What croaks like a frog, has a face like a horse, eats bananas, and hangs upside down by its toes?

Answer: A male Hammer headed Fruit Bat of Africa. He croaks constantly—probably to attract the females.

Hammer-headed Fruit Bat

Giants of the Bat World

Have you ever heard of a *flying fox?* It's not really a fox. Foxes can't fly. A Flying Fox is really a large fruit bat.

Flying foxes are the giants of the bat world. They can be 16 inches long, and weigh about 2 pounds. Some have a wing-span of 6 feet!

Flying Foxes live in hot tropical lands, and eat fruit like mangoes and bananas, figs, and guava.

They like to be near water. Often they roost in trees in swamps, in groups of hundreds, or even thousands.

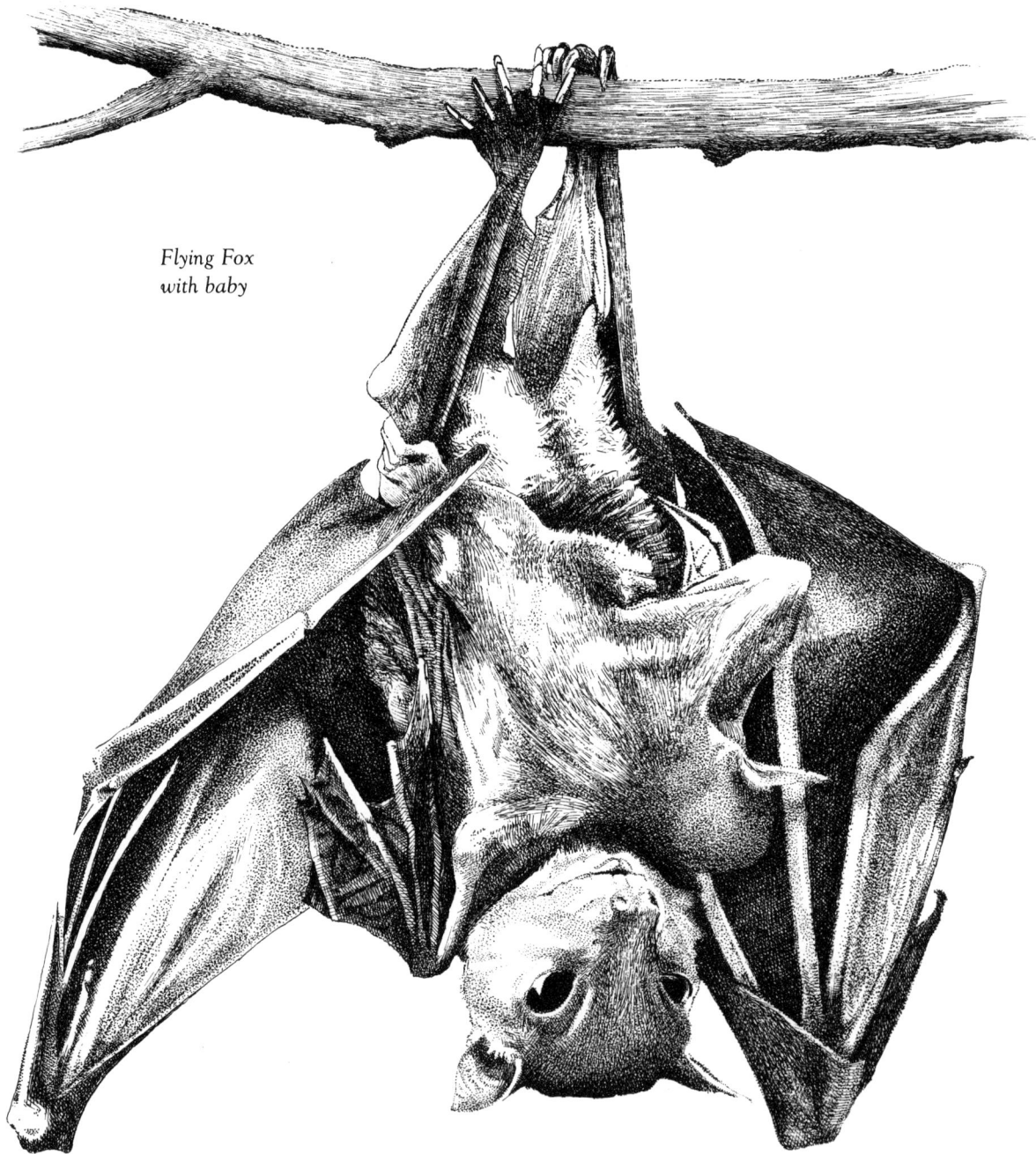

Flying Fox
with baby

When it begins to get dark, they take off for the feeding ground. Can you imagine the sky filled with hundreds of them, each with its wings spread out 5 or 6 feet?

This is how they eat. They hang on a branch with one foot, and pull the fruit close with the other foot. Then they take a bite, and squeeze the fruit in their mouths. They swallow the juice, and spit out most of the pulp. If it's a soft fruit, like banana, they'll eat the solid part, too.

After they eat for a few hours, they fly back to the roost, stopping to drink water along the way. Sometimes they drink ocean water, because their bodies need the salt.

Flying Foxes are in a group of bats called Old World Fruit Bats. These bats live only in the Eastern Hemisphere—which people often call "The Old World." They are found in Africa, Asia, and some South Sea Islands like Fiji, Tonga, and Samoa.

Here, in the Western Hemisphere—the New World—there are other kinds of fruit bats that live in Central and South America, Mexico, and warmer parts of the United States. But there are no Flying Foxes here.

Two things are special about Old World Fruit Bats.

Most bats have just the thumb claw sticking out. But many Old World Fruit Bats have two claws sticking out—the thumb claw and a claw from the second finger as well.

And—look at this close-up.

What do you notice?

This bat has large eyes.

Unlike other bats, most Old World Fruit Bats do not use echo-location. They guide themselves with their eyes. They often also locate fruit in the dark by its smell. This is true of the

Old World Fruit Bat,
with detail of eye

Hammer-headed Fruit Bat.

There are about 130 different kinds of Old World Fruit Bats, and not all of them are as large as the Flying Fox. Some are just 2 or 3 inches long. The Little Flying Cow—even though it doesn't eat fruit—is also in this group of bats, and does not use echo-location.

What Do Bats Do When It Gets Cold?

Flying Foxes always live in the tropics—where fruit keeps ripening all year round. In fact, most bats live in the warmer parts of the world. But not all of them do. Some live in cold places. There are bats in the northern part of the United States, in Canada, and even Alaska. There are bats in Denmark and France and Germany, where it's cold for part of the year. What do these bats do when the cold weather and snow make it hard to find food?

Some of them migrate. They make a yearly

trip to a warmer climate, sometimes flying hundreds of miles, even over mountains. In spring, when it gets warmer, they return, often to the same roosting place year after year.

Other bats do something else.

They hibernate.

They find a hidden dark place. It could be a hollow tree, or a cave. There, hanging by their toes, they go into a special kind of deep sleep called *hibernation*.

Hibernation is deeper than a deep sleep. The whole body slows up. The heart beats slower. The body temperature gets very low.

When a bat is awake and active, it has a normal body temperature that is the same as ours. It's about 98 degrees Fahrenheit (about 40 degrees Celsius). But when a bat is hibernating, its body temperature drops to about 45 degrees F. (around 8 degrees C). In spring, when it's warm again, the bats wake up, and go about their business.

When bats sleep every day in their roost, their body temperature gets somewhat lower, but not as low as when they hibernate.

What Do You Think About Bats?

People believe some funny things about bats. Like: IF YOU EAT FLYING FOXES, IT WILL CURE BALDNESS. Or, EATING BATS WILL IMPROVE YOUR EYESIGHT.

IF YOU PUT A BAT ON YOUR BABY'S CRADLE, THE BABY WILL SLEEP ALL DAY, LIKE A BAT.

IT'S GOOD LUCK TO CATCH A BAT IN YOUR HAT.

IF A BAT FLIES INTO YOUR HOUSE, IT BRINGS BAD LUCK.

BATS ARE GHOSTS.

Do you think these things are true?

Lots of people don't like bats and are afraid of them. Maybe it's because we don't know much about them. Or, maybe it's because the places we're likely to come across them—a dark cave, or the woods at night—are a little scary to begin with. Also, there are so many scary bat stories we see and read, we get to be afraid of them for no good reason.

The truth is, most bats are harmless little things. And, often they do things that help us. They eat pests like cockroaches and termites and scorpions. They eat insects that harm crops. The flower feeding bats help to spread pollen around. This makes more flowers grow.

And we use bat droppings (it is called "guano") as fertilizer, because it helps plants and crops grow. In New Mexico, there are huge underground caves called Carlsbad Caverns, where millions of bats have roosted. Thou-

49

sands of truckloads of bat guano have been taken out of there and used as fertilizer.

Still, it's not a great idea to try and catch a bat and take it home as a pet. A bat can have a disease called rabies. If you are bitten by a bat that happens to have rabies, or if you even have a little scratch on your hands that touches the saliva of a bat that has rabies, you can get the disease. If this happens, you have to get anti-rabies shots from the doctor. If you don't, you could die. Most bats do not have rabies. But you do not want to take a chance. So, remember—don't play around with wild bats!

Bats live a long life, for such a small animal. Mice and other small animals may live about one year. The tiny bat can often live for 25 years or even more.

But bats do have enemies that kill them. Birds of prey, like the hawk, eat bats. So do snakes. Bats are sometimes even eaten by other bats.

And now there is a new enemy that kills bats. It's not a living thing. It's pesticides—the poisonous chemicals farmers spray on crops to kill insects that destroy the crops. An insect may not die immediately. And if it is eaten by a bat, the poison then enters the bat's system. When a mother bat nurses her baby, the poison is in her milk. The small baby bat is killed by it. Millions of bats are dying this way.

One of the bad things about using pesticides is that indirectly they end up killing many different creatures other than the ones meant to be killed. In this case, the pesticides are killing the very animals—bats—who would help get rid of the insects in a natural way. So, in the end, it is even worse for the farmer. For with fewer bats around, insects thrive even more.

Bats have lived on earth for about 50 million years. They did not die out, as many animals did. Instead, there got to be more of them—different species—kinds that could live in all kinds of places; in jungles and cities, in forests and deserts.

There are around 800 different kinds of bats we know about. And we are still discovering others that we hadn't even known about before.

Index

MIRIAM SCHLEIN is the author of more than 60 books for children, many of which were Junior Literary Guild selections. These books include picture books, concept books, and natural science books. Ms. Schlein lives in New York City.

WALTER KESSELL studied art at the Rhode Island School of Design and the Paier School of Illustration. Mr. Kessell previously illustrated *The Pathless Woods,* published by Lippincott, and other children's books. He lives in Connecticut, where he works as a free-lance illustrator.

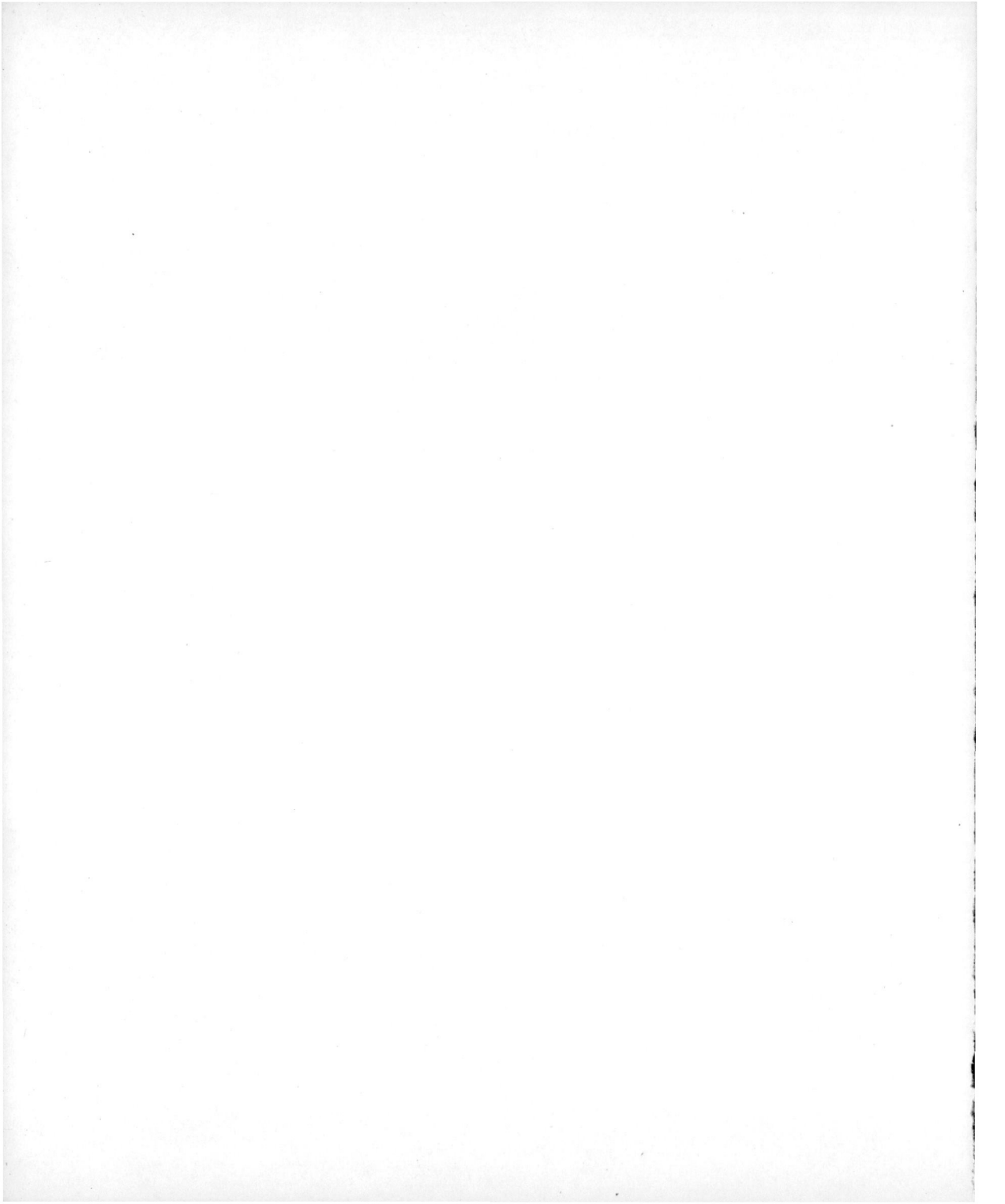